choosing

MAQSUD. S. KAROLY

(Master in Electrical Engineering)

choosing engineering as a career

(Career Guidance)

Author & Publisher:

Maqsud.S.Karoly, maqsudsk@gmail.com

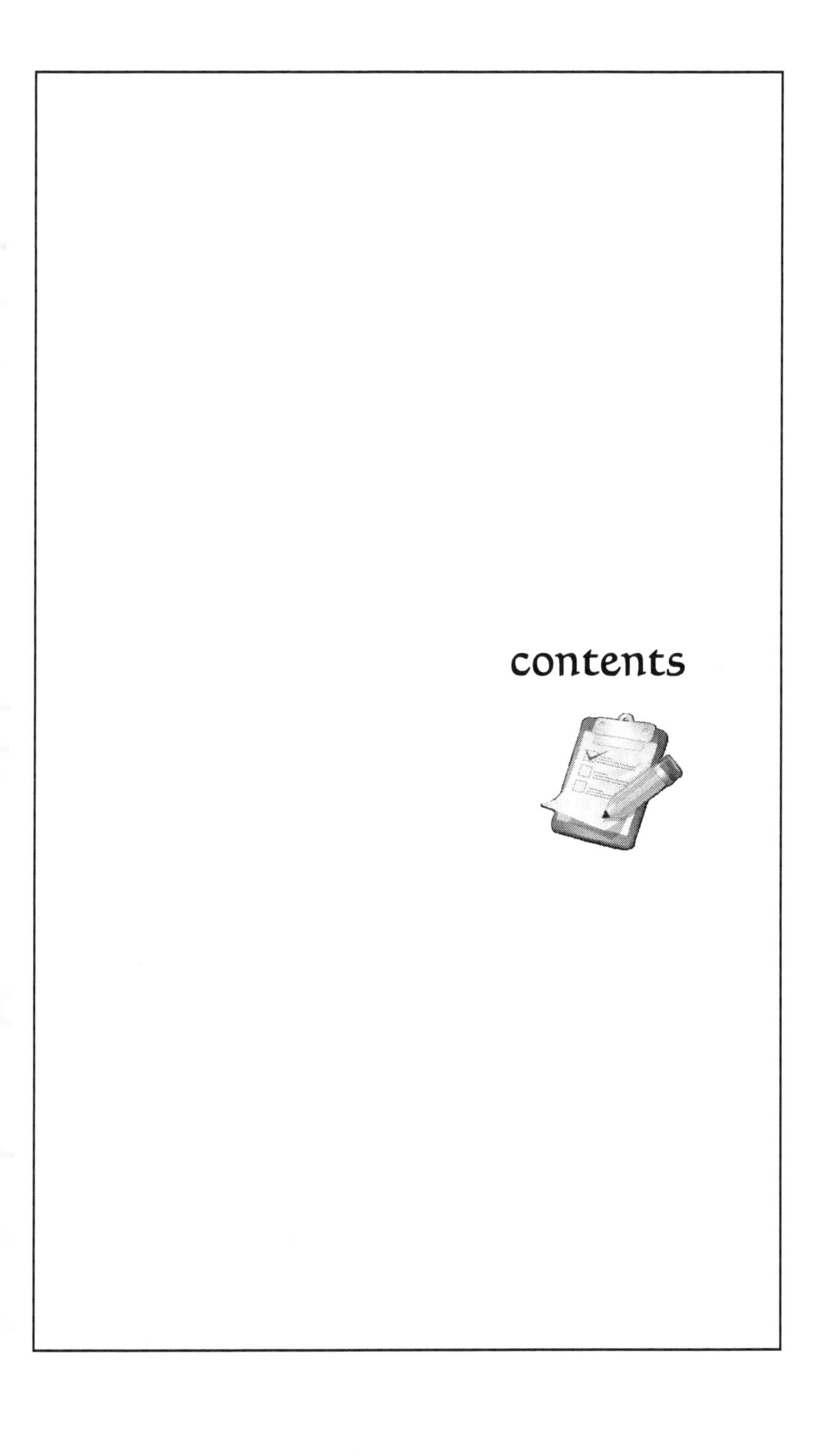

contents

Contents

Preface

It is a fact that choosing engineering as a career has not received proper treatment in career guidance, the importance of which cannot however be overestimated. Even though many career guides lists and overviews the major engineering branches, they do not provide enough information or insight to help make a well-informed decision making. This has prompted this author, who hails from an engineering background, to bring out this comprehensive and simple-to-read career guide based on first hand information and personal experiences for career aspirants to know and understand engineering closely enough to make a well-educated career decision.

It is the earnest hope and belief of the author that this guide will be of help in guiding the youngsters in taking the right decisions and saving a few careers.

introduction

Introduction

Choosing a career should not have been a hard one. Psychological theories about personality and child development like Transactional Analysis (TA) suggest that a person knows what he/she is even at a very young age. But unfortunately still too many people - in fact a majority of us - find themselves in the wrong career. How does this happen? This could have been avoided had we learned to look into ourselves rather than at others.

Every career has its own pros and cons. No career is superior over others or is a surefire to secure our future. Ending up in a career not in line with our temperament and characteristic traits can lead to life-long frustration, under-achievement and unhappiness. So the failure to look into ourselves blinded by the glint and glitter of a career may lock us in the dark realities behind when it is too late to go back. So this makes one' s career choice a choice of the life time.

So the question which career to choose is a matter of courage. It is the courage to admit what oneself is, the courage to admit that the future is not in our hands, and the courage to go for even a less lucrative or less "prestigious" career if it is indeed one 's true call. To aid this choice, with a focus on engineering, is what this guide aims for.

Engineering is surely a great career option. It is a sublime knowledge and practice which greatly influences our life. It is the most sophisticated and lucrative body of knowledge than any other. But choosing engineering as a career choice is something to be done carefully. More often than not the students end up making wrong decisions; by the time that realization dawns it will be too late to change the track, resulting in mediocrity, work-dissatisfaction, frustration and under-achievement.

Here two crucial questions come to the fore. First, who should go for engineering in the first place? Second, how to choose the engineering specialty best matching with one 's aptitude and interest?

Even though this guide primarily deals with choosing between engineering streams, the first question addressed – whether to go for engineering in the first place – too deserves one 's serious consideration. The point to be emphasize is that it is not worth to lose a great politician, thinker, speaker, artist, lawyer, singer, writer or diplomat for a mediocre engineer. So it should not happen later that one discovers that he/she is better suited for other careers and regret about it.

The next crucial factor, but that is one routinely overlooked, is the suitability of a particular engineering branch to a candidate in terms of his aptitude as well its scope for employment. Engineering compasses a variety of streams ranging from the conventional branches like Civil, Mechanical and Electrical Engineering to the latest Mechatronics, Bio-Informatics and Nanotechnology. But Studies show that *one-fourth of engineering students study in branches that do not match their interest and aptitude.*

This could undoubtedly spell trouble in one 's career in the long run. A person who would have otherwise become a great civil engineer with many grandiose projects to his credit may struggle with electronics, and may not be able excel in that field despite any amount of hard work. This may lead to mediocrity, work-dissatisfaction, frustration and under-achievement. Hence this decision is crucial, for it can make or mar the future of even bright youngsters.

In fact the prevalent system must take much of the blame for this undesirable situation. The engineering institutions generally require the students to declare their branch at the very beginning of their course itself. Ideally this should be deferred until the end of their first or even second year of study. The first one or two years should be devoted to gaining an overview of engineering and should cover the major fields available to the students, so that students are given enough time and exposure to discover their true call. There is a growing demand to make this salutary system more widespread than now.

Each engineering specialty requires distinct traits for a person to be successful in that career. A good academic record in mathematics and physics alone will not guarantee that one will excel in just any engineering field. The current practice of not taking into account the natural abilities, learning capacity and career objectives of the candidate in choosing an engineering course is undesirable. Such a choice may not only be out of sync with the personality traits of the student, and may also not indicate the actual scope which the various engineering careers provide.

Of course, over and above the aptitude in a particular stream of engineering, the various employment scopes offered by it should also be taken into account. However the popular myth of existence of a hierarchy for various engineering branches in terms of its "scope", unrelated to the inclination of the student, needs to be corrected. It must be realized that there is nothing like an ideal career, but only an ideal choice.

This career guide attempts to arm a career aspirant with relevant information to make a well-informed and meaningful career choice in engineering. The overview of engineering as well as the various engineering branches has been given in this career guide to give a panoramic view of the engineering profession to the career aspirants and enable them make informed career decisions. A few useful tips too have been provided to help the undergraduate student make his engineering course a successful one and come out with flying colors.

I would like to know if this guide has helped you in getting more insights into engineering career and making a good career choice. I welcome your feedback and suggestions for improvement at my email, mskaroly@gmail.com

welcome to engineering

Welcome to Engineering

Scientists study the world as it is; engineers create the world that has never been. — ***Theodore von Kármán***

The American Society for Engineering Education defines Engineering thus:

Engineering is the profession in which a knowledge of the mathematical and natural sciences gained by study, experience and practice is applied with judgment to develop ways to utilize the materials and forces of nature economically for benefit of mankind.

Engineering is in fact the bridge between the science and technology, the theory and the practice, the abstract and the concrete. It is an endeavor to improve our standard of living by putting our knowledge of natural laws into practice. It is a pursuit to use the principles of electricity to dispel darkness by light (here literally rather than metaphorically), the principles of aerodynamics to make globe-trotting possible, the theory of semiconductors to make mobile communication and internet feasible and the principles of biochemistry to create life-saving drugs.

Engineers design, develop and build machinery and complex systems used in the production of the bulk of consumer and industrial goods. They are instrumental in the development of buildings, highways, transportation systems and whatever like that you can think of. An engineer also has to make ensure that the finished product is effective, reliable, safe, cost efficient and environment friendly. Apart from design and development engineering professionals are also engaged in testing, producing and maintaining activities. Engineers also work in management or sales where technical knowledge and analysis is required.

Engineering had started aforetime; among its first milestones includes fundamental inventions such as the pulley, lever, and wheel. However the rise of engineering as a profession dates back only to the eighteenth century, and it made possible the industrial revolution whose profound role in changing the profile of the human civilization is well-known. Alessandro Volta, Michael Faraday, George Ohm, James Watt and Wright Brothers are some of the immortal names the world remembers with the genesis of engineering.

Even though there are numerous subdivisions for engineering, all of them can be associated with a few fundamental branches based on talent criteria, academic syllabus and work nature. A person who has studied a fundamental branch can normally pursue higher studies and job in any of its associated branches. For example mechanical engineers can go for jobs in aeronautical, production, industrial and marine engineering and so on. For this reason only the basic branches has been overviewed in this career guide in order to minimize the volume of material required for making an wise career choice.

How is engineering studies different from other fields?

Learning engineering fundamentally differs from humanities or theoretical sciences like Physics or Chemistry, even though it is closer to the latter group. This is understandable, as has been mentioned in the Introduction of this book, each profession calls for distinct characteristic traits and talent. So, one cannot master engineering concepts and practice with a similar approach to language, history or law, or even theoretical physics. This is a very important fact, as a wrong approach will prove costly, and results in wastage of precious time, effort and opportunities.

To illustrate this aspect, consider how an electronic maintenance technician works. How the circuits and components work is often of least importance for him. Mostly he works by trial and error method, testing and replacing components and tracing the circuit as per the design diagram. This is true for most engineering situations, as engineers have to learn to work with systems they don 't fully understand about, but be able to " make things work ".

This is also true for engineering theory to a great extent. An engineer is concerned more about "*what*" a device does rather than "*how*". To him every entity or system is a black box with inputs and outputs. He is worried only about the inputs and outputs, rather than what is there inside the black box, and where to fit it in his schematic to achieve his objective. In practice this black box is nothing but the device model available in the market.

For example, an electronics engineer knows that a transistor is used to amplify signals. But he need not worry about *how* transistor amplifies signals. While a Physicist may ponder over the dynamics of electrons and so on during this process, the engineer is concerned with the "useful" aspect, which is its practical utility. So he will be interested in the models of transistors available in the market, their physical characteristics, industrial applications and so on, rather than abstract concepts on transistor theory.

Where as the Physics student focuses on learning abstract physical laws and solving complex problems the engineer is concerned with how to choose components and how to install them, often based on thumb rules rather than any detailed calculation or theoretical analysis. This makes practical experience highly relevant for engineers, as it is imperative that they be exposed to the components and practices prevalent in the industry.

While maintaining that an engineering is practice-oriented, it must be reiterated that theory too has a significant role. Engineering academic syllabus is heavily loaded with theoretical concepts of a complex nature. Even though it is true that not much of that is required for most practicing engineers, except for post graduation, doctorate or research, still most selection tests are also based on theory. So one should not under-estimate the need for a strong foundation in mathematics and physics for pursuing an engineering curriculum.

Social and Cultural profile of Engineering

Engineering is a well-respected and well-paid profession with the highest employment opportunities. Unlike pure sciences which are mostly bookish and research-oriented, engineering stresses on practice and application and hence acts as a bridge between academic knowledge and the common man. For this reason engineering expertise backed by adequate experience is worth in gold, and never goes out of demand.

It goes without saying that Engineering design is a very powerful tool to make changes to environment, society and economies, and its application brings with it a great responsibility. Every product or construction used by modern society will have been influenced by engineering design. Engineering is a key driver of human development, and is essential for any country to develop crucial infrastructure and sustainable technological development.

On the flip side engineering has been sometimes seen as a somewhat dry, uninteresting field in popular culture. One difficulty in increasing public awareness of the profession is that average people, in the typical run of ordinary life, do not ever have any personal dealings with engineers, even though they benefit from their work every day. For this reason while novels and cinemas regularly characterize lawyers, doctors, police men and politicians, rarely do an engineer come up, even as a villain (except for science fiction which too tend to portray them as nerds!).

The truth is while you can' t replace a writer or artist, you can often replace an engineer. A plant will continue to run no matter who operate it, but only an Abraham Lincoln can deliver a Gettysburg address. This facet of engineering is associated with the fact that engineering deals with natural laws and things rather than ideas and people. This aspect is also something to be considered while contemplating engineering as a career choice by people with creativity in other fields.

is engineering for me?

Is Engineering for me?

Whether to go for engineering or not entirely depends upon your personality type, intellectual profile and goals. So you have to take stock of your abilities, skills and interests, identify your personality type, and match them with the appropriate job profile. In general, if you are the type of person who enjoys taking things apart and putting them back together as well as figuring out how things work, and is serious about studying, you are a strong candidate for engineering.

It goes without saying that you should be good in mathematics and Physics to pursue engineering. Because engineers spend much of their time solving problems, a strong engineering candidate should enjoy and excel at problem solving in physics and mathematics, especially on topics in his field of interest. This is all the more so since most of the selection tests for engineering jobs are problematic in nature. A flair for graphics, drafting, and design and proficiency with computers are helpful as well.

At the same time one *should primarily have the knack to make things work*, because that is what that counts in the field of work. Engineering differs from pure sciences in that it emphasizes on the practical aspects rather than theory, and bookish knowledge have little relevance in engineering practice. Engineering is about getting things done; in the actual field of work there may be no reference book that gives you the step-by-step procedure to tackle the specific problem you have on hand, or a professor you can seek guidance from. So it is the " doers " that count here without much regard to the underlying theory. Everyone may not have the innate ability to make drawings or work with gadgets and circuits.

Maintenance is the most essential aspect of an engineer 's work and he has to make sure that equipment and machines in his industrial institution are kept functional at all times. To accomplish this one should have an aptitude for making things work. Aptitude denotes an individual's ability to learn or to develop proficiency easily and quickly in an area, if provided with appropriate education or training. *It is important to realize that the engineering training cannot make up for one 's absolute lack of flair in a trade*, but only helps to polish or at the most bring out his latent talents and empower him with information to put that talent to effective use.

Where do you fit in?

While some people may be good at working with hands, others may find pleasure in reading or writing topics of their interest, and still others prefer to work with people rather than things. Psychologists have divided the activities people enjoy doing and are good at indicative of their talents into four categories: things or objects, data or information, ideas and expression, and people. Different combinations of these basic interest and aptitudes have been worked out to identify different types of people and the kinds of careers whey would be suitable. These include the technically inclined people, the abstract thinkers, artistic and creative types of people, the social type of persons and the conventional people.

As for an engineering candidate, the world of objects and things should be very important to him. Rather than pondering over ideas or laboring over art, or impress people with one' s communication, management and public speaking skills, what we need for engineering are realistic people who are good at mechanical jobs, like to work with things rather than people. (For people of other categories there are even better career options than engineering available). It would be well that you make introspection and discover your true call, preferably by undertaking a psychometric test like Differential Aptitude Test (DAT).

Consider other options too

To study engineering just for the sake of an engineering degree is not an attractive proposition today. Earning money is not the sole objective of a career, but work satisfaction and personal accomplishments too counts a lot. Moreover rather than a degree, it is a respectable job that one should look forward. Considering that a vast number of engineering graduates work in fields unrelated to their study due to lack of ample opportunities, this point needs to be emphasized over and again.

Today there is growing awareness and interest about exciting careers in humanities, pure sciences, commerce, civil services, law and management and the career choices have been increasingly shifting in favor of non-engineering disciplines. Those without any particular talent in engineering but have a marked flair and interest for other areas like literature, history, art, psychology or fashion designing are strongly advised not to take up engineering.

It must be realized that being a discipline concerned with things rather than people, *an engineering career doesn't hold the potential to "influence" people, lead people, make changes in the society or become famous like a writer, lawyer or politician.* It is also to be observed that many influential administrative positions in the society too are not associated with engineering.

choosing an engineering major

How to Choose an Engineering Major?

The question " What discipline to choose? " is as crucial as the question "Whether to choose engineering? " The main factors to be considered in choosing an engineering discipline are the following.

Aptitude:

The general rule is that one should opt for a field for which one had displayed a natural inclination even in his/her early life. It easily strikes anyone that a person who wishes to pursue Architecture should possess a fairly good drawing skill and aesthetic sense. Similar is the case with any other branch; an electrical or electronic engineering aspirant should have talent to work with electrical gadgets and wiring connections, and a mechanical engineering aspirant should do well with mechanical devices.

Intuitive Nature of the Subject:

An engineering stream like electronics or electrical engineering has concepts that are least intuitive unlike say civil or mechanical engineering. For example while it is quite straightforward to understand how mechanical devices work, it is not that easy to comprehend how the electronic circuits work. Hence the choice of a branch should be based on one 's learning capacity.

In no way it is implied that such left brain oriented branches are " superior " to other more intuitive ones, for opportunities and other merits are not necessarily related to that factor. The fact that civil engineering, despite being less technical and more intuitive than electronics provides better job prospects than the latter gives ample testimony to this.

Opportunities in the Public Sector:

The public sector enterprises like railways and heavy industries routinely calls graduates in certain engineering disciplines like electrical and mechanical engineering in bulk numbers. This is not true for many other engineering disciplines like Biotechnology or Architecture. However it should be borne in mind that the opportunities in the public sector are scarce and the competition for them is of an extreme kind; so this factor may not be taken as a major consideration unless one is very serious about it.

Opportunities Abroad:

The opportunities abroad too should be similarly considered by those dreaming or planning to go overseas.

Dependence on Industry for Jobs:

One particular factor of interest, especially in the perspective of the number of job opportunities, is the **role of industry** in providing jobs. Certain engineering disciplines, for example mechanical and electrical engineering, heavily rely on the industry to provide jobs to its exponents. So the potential for such jobs depends on the existence of industries and the industrial atmosphere in your state, unless you are willing to move out. Considering that such technical knowledge usually have little relevance outside the industry, such paths should be tread with caution.

Opportunities for the Fresh Graduates:

One important criterion to judge an engineering field is the availability of job **opportunities for fresh graduates**. The problem is all the more acute for mechanical, electrical and electronics engineering etc, which generally pertain to the industry. Normally the existing industries prefer only experienced hands for their vacancies. So the vast majority of the graduates in these disciplines may find it tough to make a breakthrough. On the other hand this is less of a problem in streams like IT or civil engineering, which provides abundant number of job opportunities. The **percentage of graduates** in a discipline employed in their same field of study is similar index of its employment scope.

Industry-Academia Gap:

The industry-academia gap in the engineering curriculum is a reality, and in fact cannot be bridged beyond a certain extent, and as a result there is a wide chasm between what is learned at the institution and what has to be actually accomplished in the field. As a result without supplementary training and adequate experience in the industry the graduates cannot deliver at the workplace. This factor is also of interest, being non-uniform among the various engineering branches.

" IT-Friendliness ":

Today is the era of Information Technology, which is the largest job-provider today, in fact even for engineering graduates from non-IT streams. Even though ideally an engineering graduate should be working in the field of his study, more often than not he might be forced to migrate to IT due to scarcity of opportunities there. However all engineering branches are not preferred to the same degree by the IT companies owing to the differences in the applicability of their technical nature to IT, with the circuit branches being favored than others. The crucial aspect of "**IT-friendliness**" also should be compared.

Scope for Private Practice:

One major attribute and attraction tagged to an engineering career is the scope for **private practice**. It is well known that certain fields like civil and architecture provide ample scope for private practice. However even though almost all engineering branches have the potential to offer scope for private practice, in actuality not all of them do so. We should look into that too.

Pace of domain transition:

This being a fast changing world, the information in every field is undergoing **fast transitions** and paradigm changes. Even though this is in general applicable to all engineering branches, still there is wide difference in the susceptibility of the various engineering branches to the onslaught of new information. The relatively new branches like IT epitomize this aspect, while the conventional branches like civil or mechanical engineering are not subjected to such fast changes. Such revamps have some inherent disadvantages and may not be welcome for everyone, as it would easily render much hard learned things obsolete or of no use frequently and also would demand constant updating on the part of the practitioner. Only the initiated will be interested in such a challenge.

Work Nature of the Job:

The number of hours of work expected, the sedentary nature of the job, the need for outdoor field work, etc too should be considered.

overview of engineering specialties

Note: *As this book has been written for an international audience, the details of courses outlined are generic in nature, and the reader should refer to the standards in his own country for more details.*

civil engineering

CIVIL ENGINEERING

Overview:

Working in one of the largest branches of engineering, civil engineers deal with buildings, bridges, dams, roads, and other structures. They plan, design, and supervise the construction of facilities such as high-rise buildings, airports, water treatment centers, and sanitation plants. Rather than just building structures civil engineers have on hand a more sublime objective - advancing civilization and building our quality of life.

Civil engineering is about community service, development, and improvement -- the planning, design, construction, and operation of facilities essential to modern life. Civil engineers are problem solvers, meeting the challenges of pollution, traffic congestion, drinking water and energy needs, urban redevelopment, and community planning.

As the technological revolution expands, as the world's population increases, and as environmental concerns mount, the civil engineer will perform a vital role in improving quality of life for the 21st century and help make our world a better place to live. Civil engineering offers a wide range of career choices in design, construction, research, teaching, or management.

Civil Engineering is very a diverse and dynamic field grouped into several major divisions of engineering like structural, environmental, geotechnical, water resources, transportation, construction and urban planning.

Job Prospects

Civil engineers are employed by government as well as private sectors for construction works in the fields of Public Works, airports, harbors, ports, with water and sewage boards, railways, private construction companies, military engineering services, consultancy services etc.

Curriculum

Civil engineering course is designed to introduce concepts in structures, foundation, surveying, construction, hydraulics and environmental engineering, works management and cost, transportation engineering, irrigation engineering etc.

Aptitude Required

The concepts are intuitive and not of a highly mathematical or technical nature since energy conversions are not much involved; so most people can study and practice this field comfortably. It would be helpful to have good drawing and visualizing skill to excel in this field. At the high school level one should be interested and comfortable with the following subjects:

- Trigonometry
- Geometry
- Statics

Talent Check

- Have you got the talent to draw buildings and other structures?
- While building your new home did you use to give your own suggestions?
- Get the building plan of your house. Are you able to follow it? Can you suggest any improvements in it?

Review

Civil Engineering is the oldest and the "real" engineering field. Due to its high application, since construction is ubiquitous, Civil Engineering provides the highest number of job openings after IT anywhere in the world. Fresh graduates can find job and work experience comparatively easily. It provides excellent scope for people-management with large number of engineers, supervisors and laborers coming under a project leader. It also provides very good opportunities for experienced persons even after retirement, as project leaders etc. There are also ample opportunities for private practice, self-employment, contract work and real-estate business in Civil Engineering.

Civil Engineering- Synopsis

Aptitude:

Skill, imagination and aesthetic sense for drawing buildings and other structures.

Foundation:

Good foundation in trigonometry, geometry and statics.

Positive Aspects:

- The oldest and the "real" engineering field.
- Concepts are intuitive and not of a highly mathematical or technical nature.
- Updating of knowledge is less required.
- Less indoor or lab work involved.
- Highest number of job openings after IT all over the world, since construction is ubiquitous.
- Highest percentage of graduates employed in the same field of study after IT.
- Job opportunities don't depend on the presence of industry.
- Opportunities for fresh graduates to find jobs are highest, after IT.
- Ample opportunities for private practice, self-employment, contract work and real-estate business.
- Very good scope for experienced persons even after retire-

ment, as project leaders etc.

- Opportunities in design using CAD.
- Even those who are not technically inclined can succeed or at least survive.
- Provides ample scope for man-management with large number of engineers, supervisors, laborers etc coming under a project leader.

Negative Aspects:

- Civil engineering graduates are not preferred by IT industry unlike graduates in circuit branches.
- Needs outdoor field work. (But this may be a welcome thing for the outgoing type of people).
- Less frequently called for by the public sector and industries than electrical/mechanical engineers.
- Limited opportunities in industries.

mechanical engineering

MECHANICAL ENGINEERING

(Aeronautical, Production, Industrial, Ship technology, Marine Engineering, Mechatronics, Robotics)

Overview

Mechanical engineering is one of the largest, broadest, and oldest engineering disciplines. Mechanical engineers use the principles of energy, materials, and mechanics to design and manufacture machines and devices of all types. They create the processes and systems that drive technology and industry. If you have a fascination for things that move -- cars, trains, planes, spacecraft, amusement park rides - then you are a strong candidate for mechanical engineering.

Mechanical engineers research, develop, design, manufacture, and test tools, engines, machines, and other mechanical devices. They work internal combustion engines, steam and gas turbines, refrigeration and air-conditioning equipment, machine tools, material handling systems, elevators and escalators, industrial production equipment, and robots used in manufacturing. Mechanical engineers also design tools that other engineers need for their work. However it may be noted that due to the notion that the coursework involves lot of physical activity - which is true to an extent - mechanical engineering is not preferred by females in general.

Aeronautical engineers are concerned with the design and maintenance, construction, testing and operation of aircraft and aircraft components. The main thrust in this area is on the design and development, which even extends to space and satellite research.

Production and Industrial engineers aim at higher productivity by adopting integrated design and efficient planning of operative systems. The work involves the design and installation of integrated systems for men, materials, equipment and process for increasing the productivity of goods and detailing the optimum quality which is economically viable. They are concerned with planning, measuring and controlling all activities within the organization, besides designing the production process for a product.

Automobile Engineers are concerned with designing, planning, manufacturing, repairing, maintaining and upgradation of all moving vehicles such as cars, trucks, motorcycles, scooters etc. Automobile engineers design new models of cars, keeping in view their performance, capacity, durability, beauty and cost for both manufacture and maintenance. With increasing concern for pollution and fuel efficiency, these engineers also set the standards of quality in such matters.

Acquiring a basic degree in Mechanical engineering and then going for specialization in automobile engineering is possible.

Marine Engineers are responsible for the safe running of all engines, boilers, refrigerating and sanitary equipments, deck machinery and steam connection of marine ships, and the maintenance, repair and construction of all marine machinery. This also includes the supervision of engine crew involved in operating the machines and checking for smooth functioning of all steam engines, electric motors, propulsive engines etc.

Mechatronics is the synergistic combination of precision mechanical engineering, electronic control, computer technology and a systems approach in the design of products and processes. It compasses many new developments such as Internet control of machines, autonomous robots and engine management systems. Mechatronics students must have a strong background of Mechanical Engineering, with a good working knowledge of Electrical, Computer, and Systems Design Engineering.

Mechatronics graduates are expected to be employed in all sectors of manufacturing, electrical and electronics industry — product design, manufacturing, system design, equipment and system control, robotics, automation, computer technology, quality control, industrial management, and marketing.

Robotics is the engineering science and technology of robots, and their design, manufacture, and application. Robots can either help or take away human jobs. Robotics is related to electronics, mechanics, and software.

Today, commercial and industrial robots are in widespread use performing jobs cheaper or more accurately and reliably than humans. They are also employed for jobs which are too dirty, dangerous, or dull to be suitable for humans. Robots are widely used in manufacturing, assembly, and packing; transport; earth and space exploration; surgery; weaponry; laboratory research; safety; and mass production of consumer and industrial goods.

Robotics as an undergraduate course is rarely available. But to do Robotics later one can preferably take Mechanical engineering or Mechatronics.

Job Prospects

Mechanical engineers are absorbed in private and public sector industries where any type of manufacturing activity takes place. In the public sector they are absorbed in Public works departments, defense, railways, post and telegraph and so on. Ship technologists and marine engineers are employed in ships and merchant navy. Automobile engineers are employed by vehicle manufacturing and assembling plants, in maintenance and service stations, in private transport companies and so on. Aeronautical engineers are employed by airlines, aircraft manufacturers and other aircraft industry.

Curriculum

The core curriculum of Mechanical Engineering introduces the students to mechanics, energy and heat, thermodynamics, machine theory, mathematics, engineering sciences, design and manufacturing. Aeronautical engineering focuses on fundamentals of propulsion, electronics, automatic control guidance, theory of aerodynamics, structural analysis, material science and fluid dynamics. Production and Industrial engineering focuses on component production, process planning, production planning, systems engineering, industrial automation and process engineering besides management subjects.

Aptitude required

Concepts in Mechanical engineering are comparatively intuitive, as energy forms studied are mechanical in nature. One needs good conceptualization and drawing skills besides a genuine interest in the working of mechanical parts of pumps, vehicles etc to do well in this field. At high school level one should have done well in the following subjects:

- Calculus
- Dynamics
- Heat and Thermodynamics

Talent Check

- Have you displayed a enthusiasm to work with mechanical gadgets, using your hands, fixing things and making things work, even if it is as simple as fixing a curtain or a fitting a gas cylinder to a stove?
- When the water pump in your house or your car is not working for some minor problem do you use to bring it back into action?
- Does your mom call you first when something goes out of order?

Review

Mechanical engineering being a broad discipline provides wide opportunities in various fields. Most industries need mechanical engineers. Mechanical engineering and business are closely intertwined. Mechanical engineers have excellent scope in industrial and business management, especially if armed with a master in Business in Administration.

On the flip side job opportunities in Mechanical engineering branches depend on openings in industry, and hence the fresh graduates may find it difficult to get through. This is especially true for a specialized branch like Aeronautical engineering. The percentage of graduates employed in the same field of study is not impressive. The academia-industry gap is very high here, and without supplementary training and adequate experience in the industry the graduate cannot deliver in the field. Mechanical engineering branches provide little chance for private practice unlike civil engineering etc.

Mechanical Engineering Branches - Synopsis

Aptitude:

- Good conceptualization and drawing skills of mechanical parts, vehicles etc.
- Interest in the working of mechanical parts of pumps, vehicles etc.

Foundation:

- Strong foundation in mathematics and physics, especially Calculus, Dynamics, heat and thermodynamics etc.

Positive Aspects:

- Good number of opportunities for experienced engineers in places with good industrial presence.
- Mechanical engineering graduates are frequently called in public sector including heavy industries, Railways etc.
- Mechanical engineers have wide scope in ship technology, marine engineering, aeronautical engineering etc.
- Most industries need mechanical engineers.
- Opportunities in design and programming with Ansys, Pro-E, Auto-Cad etc.
- Concepts are intuitive, even though their quantitative treatment is certainly involved.
- Mechanical engineering and business are closely inter-

twined. So Mechanical engineers have excellent scope in industrial and business management, especially if armed with an MBA.

- Self-employment is possible by setting up garages or workshops.

Negative Aspects:

- Not generally preferred by females
- Job opportunities depend on openings in industry.
- The percentage of graduates employed in the same field of study is not large.
- Limited opportunities for fresh graduates.
- The academia-industry gap is very high here, and without supplementary training and adequate experience in the industry the graduate cannot deliver in the field.
- Mechanical engineering graduates are not preferred by IT industry unlike graduates in circuit branches.
- Little chance for private practice unlike civil engineering etc.
- Mechanical engineering curriculum demands high infrastructural investments in labs and workshops.

electrical engineering

ELECTRICAL ENGINEERING

Overview:

Even though Electrical and electronics engineering have a lot in common, in some places they are taught as two separate streams- one is "Electrical" or "Electrical and Electronics Engineering", while the other is the "Electronics" or "Electronics and Communication Engineering". The former concentrates mainly on the conventional electrical engineering whereas the latter fully focuses on the Electronics and communication technologies.

Whereas usually Electronics Engineers deal with micro and low power circuitry and equipments, the electrical engineers are concerned with bulk power and its handling, and the associated equipments like generators, transformers, transmission lines, induction motors etc. Mostly they are concerned with providing and maintaining electric supply to industries and institutions, designing, testing and installing substations and power systems, computerized monitoring of electric power systems using SCADA, control and automation of processes using PLC and so on.

Some of the equipment that electrical engineers routinely handle includes electric motors, machinery controls, lighting and wiring in buildings, power generating, controlling, and transmission devices used by electric utilities. Many electrical engineers also work in areas closely related to computers.

Job Prospects

Electrical engineers find jobs in the public and private sector in the fields of electrical design, installation and maintenance of electrical installations and substations. They are employed by power plants, electricity boards, large institutions, railways and so on. There are good opportunities in for experienced engineers all over the world in the power as well as communication technologies. Most of the openings in public sector for electronics graduates are open to electrical graduates too.

Curriculum

Core courses taken by electrical engineering students include such topics as circuits, machines, electrical energy systems, electrical protection systems, control systems, and electronics.

Aptitude Required:

Electrical Engineering heavily relies on mathematics, electric circuit theories and electronics to explain the relations between electrical and other forms of energy. One should also definitely have aptitude for making and checking electrical wiring connections as well as an interest in the working of and knack for repairing electrical equipments, switchboard connections etc to be successful in this field. At the high school level one should do well in the following subjects:

- Calculus
- Electromagnetic Induction
- Electricity and Magnetism
- AC circuit Analysis

Talent Check

Note: The following checks are meant for only contemplation and need not be attempted in practice.

- Do you have the urge to check your main-switch when the power goes down in your house (or just wait for the electrician to come!) ? Suppose if one phase is not there can you give power to that circuit from one of the live phases?
- Unscrew one wall switchboard in your house and look behind it. Can you recognize the wiring connections provided therein? Can you think about interchanging switches of any two appliances?
- Get the electrical wiring diagram of your house. Are you able to follow it? Can you modify it by assuming that there is an additional room in your house?

Review

Electrical engineering graduates can seek career as well as higher studies in diverse fields like electrical, electronics, computer, instrumentation and control, optoelectronics, and all related fields. However the job-opportunities in Electrical Engineering depend on the presence of industry. Hence fresh graduates will find it difficult to find an opening. Unfortunately the academia-industry gap is very high in this field, and without supplementary training and adequate experience in the industry the graduate cannot deliver in the field. The percentage of graduates in electrical engineering employed in the same field of study is quite low. Electrical engineering provides little scope for private practice unlike civil engineering.

Electrical Engineering - Synopsis

Aptitude:

- Making and checking electrical wiring connections
- Interest in the working of and knack for repairing electrical equipments, switchboard connections etc.

Foundation:

- Particularly strong foundation in mathematics, especially calculus, Laplace transforms etc.
- Strong foundation in electric circuits and networks, magnetism, electromagnetic induction, A.C circuit analysis etc.

Positive Aspects:

- Electrical engineering graduates are frequently called by public sector including heavy industries, Railways, Electricity boards etc.
- Good number of opportunities for experienced persons.
- All industries and major establishments have electrical sections.
- Opportunities in design and programming with SCADA, PLC etc.
- Graduates are preferred by IT industry.
- Electrical engineering graduates can seek career as well as higher studies in diverse fields like electrical, electronics,

computer, instrumentation and control, optoelectronics, and all related fields.

Negative Aspects:

- Without the right aptitude, it is not advisable to take up this field since it highly relies on the left brain.
- Theoretical concepts are not intuitive unlike, say, civil or mechanical engineering.
- Consists of voluminous and involved theoretical aspects which may have little practical relevance even for most of the practicing engineers.
- Job opportunities largely depend on openings in industry, and are limited in places with little industrial presence.
- Even though electrical systems are ubiquitous the diploma holders and technicians too play major roles in them, and the role of the graduate engineer is somewhat limited.
- Chances for errors in electrical connections and hence loss of life/property to occur are always present.
- Unfortunately the academia-industry gap is very high here, and without supplementary training and adequate experience in the industry the graduate cannot deliver in the field.
- The percentage of graduates in electrical engineering employed in the same field of study is quite low.
- Job prospects for fresh graduates are limited.
- Little scope for private practice unlike civil engineering.

electronics & communication engg

ELECTRONICS & COMMUNICATION ENGG

(Instrumentation Engineering)

Overview

The Electronics engineers design, develop, test, and install electronic systems, electronic equipments and devices. Whereas the electrical engineers deal with bulk power and its handling, usually electronics engineers deals with micro and low power circuitry and equipments. From the conventional broadcast and communications systems to the global positioning system that can continuously provide the location of a vehicle electronics engineers are responsible for a wide range of technologies. Many, in fact the majority, of electronics engineers work in areas closely related to computers.

Instrumentation Engineers are responsible for the design, construction and maintenance of instruments and control systems for industries.

Job Prospects

Electronics and instrumentation engineers are called by telephone companies, airports, police wireless departments, defense etc in the public sector. They are also called by electronics industry, entertainment transmission industry and research establishments.

Curriculum

The Electronics and communication curriculum introduces the electronic networks and devices, electromagnetic field theory, digital signal processing, control systems, communication technologies, microprocessors and computer fundamentals.

Aptitude Required

Electronics & Communication consists of involved mathematical and theoretical concepts in electromagnetics, digital circuits, signal processing and other advanced topics, and highly relies on the left brain. Hence without confirmed aptitude, it is not advisable to take up this field. On the practical side one should have the ability for making and checking electrical wiring connections, interest in the working of and knack for repairing electronic equipments like radio, T.V, telephone etc and talent for assembly and working of electronic circuits on PCBs, besides logic and programming skills.

At the high school level one should be comfortable with the following subjects:

- Calculus
- Electric circuits
- AC circuit analysis
- Electromagnetic waves
- Electronics

Talent Check

- Do you use to tinker with electronic goodies like radios? Do you know about the frequency bands of the various radio stations?
- When you bought your new TV was it you who tuned the stations? Or was it you who explained your mom how to make your new microwave oven work?
- Can you troubleshoot your computer hardware or printer for at least minor problems? Are you being consulted by your friends or relatives for such needs?
- Have you successfully done any simple electronic project? If not, try to execute one electronic project from any electronics practical book, say assembling a radio, and see if you are good at it.

Review

With the globalization setting in and the state of the technologies pervading barriers more easily the scope for Electronics and communication engineers has been steadily rising. One positive aspect of electronics engineering is that graduates are highly preferred by IT industry, sometimes even more than computer science and IT graduates since ECE graduates have exposure to communication, wireless technology, embedded systems etc.

However it is also a truth that in the developing countries at the moment this field doesn ' t provide as many job opportunities as the hype around it suggest. A study in India shows that vast majority of ECE graduates migrate to IT related fields, where their technical expertise is not put to much use. The reason for this partly may be due to that many advanced technologies in Electronics and communication have not yet been firmly established there. Even though the software industry has made great strides, still hardware and semiconductor industries are lagging behind in in such countries compared to the developed ones.

Electronics & Communication Engineering - Synopsis

Aptitude:

- Making and checking electrical wiring connections
- Interest in the working of and knack for repairing electronic equipments like radio, T.V, telephone etc.
- Talent for assembly and working of simple electronic circuits on PCBs.
- Logic and Programming skills.

Foundation:

- Particularly strong foundation in mathematics
- Strong foundation in electricity and magnetism, A.C circuit analysis, electronic circuits etc.

Positive Aspects:

- Graduates are highly preferred by IT industry, sometimes even more than Computer Science and IT graduates since ECE graduates have exposure to communication, wireless technology etc.
- Electronics engineering graduates can seek career as well as higher studies in diverse fields like electronics, computer, instrumentation and control, optoelectronics, and all related fields.

Negative Aspects:

- Without the right aptitude, it is not advisable to take up this field since it highly relies on the left brain.
- Consists of highly mathematical and involved theoretical concepts.
- Theoretical concepts are least intuitive and hence " boring " unlike, say, civil or mechanical engineering.
- Job opportunities depend on openings in electronics industry, and hence the industrial profile of a country.
- Chances for errors in wiring connections and hence loss of property to occur is present.
- The academia-industry gap is very high here, and without supplementary training and adequate experience the graduate cannot deliver in the field.
- The percentage of graduates in electronics engineering employed in the same field of study is in fact the lowest (most migrate to IT field).
- Job prospects for fresh graduates in the same field of study are very limited.
- Little chance for private practice unlike civil engineering.

architecture

ARCHITECTURE

Overview

Architecture involves applying engineering principles to the construction, planning, and design of buildings and other structures. Strictly speaking there is subtle difference between an " Architect " and an "Architectural engineer ". Architects focus on function layout and aesthetics of building projects. Architectural engineers are responsible for developing the details of the building systems, including structural, heating/air conditioning, plumbing, fire protection and electrical based on the design.

The architectural engineering focuses several areas, including the structural integrity of buildings, the design and analysis of heating, ventilating and air conditioning systems, efficiency and design of plumbing, fire protection and electrical systems, acoustic and lighting planning, and energy conservation issues. Not just limited to the front elevation designs and aesthetics architecture has become a part and parcel of urban planning, turnkey housing projects, satellite townships, product designing, landscaping and construction management.

Unlike the rest of the Engineering courses of four-year duration, Architecture is of five-year duration. (" Architectural Engineering " which is a four year course, as distinct from Bachelor of

Architecture, is available too). The additional year is meant for facilitating the students to undertake a mandatory tour, to learn about the construction designs of all kinds (cultural, historical and contemporary). Along with this is a six-month practical training with an architect anywhere in the world to assess the area of their aptitude and plan their academic progression accordingly.

Curriculum

The course is holistic. It is a combination of engineering subjects and humanities, with subjects dealing with structural engineering, surveying, water supply on the technical side and those like sociology, economics, human sentiments and historical perspectives on the humanities side.

Students specializing in Architectural Engineering will explore engineering design, structures, mechanical and electrical systems, and construction management. Students will study the strength of materials, thermodynamics, fluid mechanics, electric circuits, and engineering economics. Students will also learn about the history of architectural design.

Job Prospects

Most Architectural Engineers work in the construction industry or related areas. Some Architectural Engineers are self employed. One can start his career as an assistant. The job prospects are good in places like Europe, the Middle East and Asia where there is a lot of infrastructure development.

Architecture has the scope for diversification to Web designing, cinematic backdrop, graphics, visual communication, advertisement layout designing, landscaping, interior designing, industrial designing, textile designing and so on.

Aptitude Required:

Skill, imagination and aesthetic sense for drawing buildings and other structures are prerequisites for embarking on a career in Architecture. Student should have good foundation in mathematics, especially three dimensional geometry and calculus, and statics.

At the high school level one should do well in the following topics:

- Trigonometry
- Geometry
- Statics

Talent Check

- Have you got a talent to draw buildings and other structures, and visualize three dimensional figures?
- While building your new home did you use to give your own suggestions?
- Get the building plan of your house. Are you able to follow it?

Can you suggest any improvements in it?

- It is advisable that the candidate undergoes an aptitude test in Architecture (which is mandatory in many countries) .

Review

Architecture can be a highly lucrative and satisfying career with the right aptitude. Rather than the bookish knowledge, the experience gained through various projects will be the most invaluable for an architect. But experience indicates that the architects who become really successful are quite few. Fresh graduates may initially struggle to find jobs, as the openings are not numerous. The starting salaries too are low. The assignments may entail long hours of work and concentration. If one is hardworking and have the right aptitude one can confidently step into the field.

Architecture – Synopsis

Aptitude:

- Skill, imagination and aesthetic sense for drawing buildings and other structures.

Foundation:

- Good foundation in mathematics, especially three dimensional geometry and calculus, and statics.

Positive Aspects:

- Highly lucrative and satisfying career with the right aptitude.
- Concepts are intuitive and not of a highly technical nature.
- Not much technical aptitude for hardware or lab work is required.
- Less indoor or lab work involved.
- Job opportunities don 't depend on the presence of industry.
- Ample opportunities for private practice and self-employment.
- Opportunities in design using CAD and other design software.

Negative Aspects:

- Bachelor in Architecture is of five year duration.
- Only those with aptitude can survive.
- Graduates may initially struggle to find jobs, as the openings are not numerous. The starting salaries too are low.
- Graduates in architecture are not preferred by IT industry unlike graduates in electrical branches.
- Entails long hours of work and concentration.
- Needs outdoor field work.
- Not often called by public sector.
- Little opportunities in industries.

chemical engineering

CHEMICAL ENGINEERING

(Polymer, Plastic, Textile Engineering)

Overview

Chemical engineers are experts in substances and how they react to one another or to various technical processes. Based on their deep understanding of molecules and their interactions, chemical engineers design manufacturing processes for products such as detergents, gasoline, plastics, and synthetic materials.

Chemical engineers improve food processing techniques, and methods of producing fertilizers, to increase the quantity and quality of available food. They also construct the synthetic fibers that make our clothes more comfortable and water resistant; they develop methods to mass-produce drugs, making them more affordable; and they create safer, more efficient methods of refining petroleum products, making energy and chemical sources more productive and cost effective. They also develop solutions to environmental problems, such as pollution control and remediation. And they process chemicals, which are used to make or improve just about everything you see around you.

Textile engineers are involved in the production and fabrication of different kinds of textiles. They handle the manufacturing process that converts fibre into textile and textile products, work with dyes and weaves to ensure consistency, durability and fabric strength, and develop new technologies and processes for the manufacture of natural and synthetic, durable, cost-efficient fabric. They can also work in research, and design development of new textile suitable for specific purposes, as well as upgrading of production and quality control technologies.

Job Prospects

Chemical engineers work in soap, oil, paint, pharmaceuticals, healthcare, design and construction, pulp and paper, petrochemicals, food processing, specialty chemicals, polymers, synthetic fibers, biotechnology, and environmental health and safety industries, among others.

Curriculum

The core curriculum of a chemical engineering program, in addition to topics in Mathematics, usually consists of Organic Chemistry, Mass and Energy Balances, Physics, Statistics, Physical Chemistry, Separation Processes, Transport Operations, Thermodynamics, Process, Measurements and Controls, Physical Chemistry, Chemical Process Modeling, Chemical Reactor Analysis and Design Process and Plant Design, Separation Processes, Process Materials etc.

Aptitude Required

Chemical Engineering is a combination of Chemistry, Math and certain areas of Physics. One must be genuinely interested in chemical processes and have a flair for chemical formulae and equations. At the high school one should have done well in the following areas:

- Mathematics
- Chemistry
- Thermodynamics

Talent Check

- Have you been interested in Chemistry?
- Did you do well in your Chemistry lab?
- Are you comfortable with understanding and remembering chemical formulae and processes?
- If possible try to get a chemistry set and do some simple projects

Review

Chemical Engineering provides lucrative prospects in petroleum industry, refineries etc, especially in Middle-East, textile industry and many other industries. Among manufacturing industries, pharmaceuticals may provide the best opportunities for jobseekers. Future employment growth can also be expected in service industries such as scientific research and development services, particularly in energy and the developing fields of biotechnology and nanotechnology.

On the flip side, especially in the of context many Asian countries, openings are quite limited. Fresh graduates may struggle to get a break-through. Graduates in chemical engineering are not preferred by IT industry unlike graduates in electrical branches. Unfortunately the academia-industry gap is very large here, and without supplementary training and adequate experience the graduate cannot deliver in the field. The percentage of graduates in chemical engineering employed in the same field of study is low. Chemical engineering provides little chance for private practice.

Chemical Engineering – Synopsis

Aptitude

- Ability to understand and interest in chemical reactions, memorize chemical formulae and equations.

Positive Aspects:

- Lucrative prospects in petroleum industry, refineries etc, especially in Middle-East and other such oil rich countries, and textile industry.

Negative Aspects:

- Only those with aptitude can succeed.
- Openings depends on the industrial profile of a country. Fresh graduates will struggle to get a break-through if the openings are limited.
- Graduates in chemical engineering are not preferred by IT industry unlike graduates in circuit branches.
- Not often called by public sector.
- Little opportunities in industries other than chemical and petroleum industries.
- Theoretical concepts are not intuitive unlike, say, mechanical engineering.
- Unfortunately the academia-industry gap is very high here, and without supplementary training and adequate experi-

ence the graduate cannot deliver in the field.

- The percentage of graduates in chemical engineering employed in the same field of study is low.
- Little chance for private practice.

computer science/ IT engineering

COMPUTER SCIENCE ENGINEERING / IT

Overview:

With the software boom reaching ever new heights the Computer Science Engineering and Information Technology have been the new kids on the block in the employment market. Software engineers create programs for use on various computer platforms such as Windows, Macintosh, or Unix and also develop applications for Web. They deal with all aspects of Software design life cycle including System Analysis and Design, programming, testing and trouble-shooting. Information Technology Engineers focus on creating and maintaining networks of information, often within companies or government agencies.

The CSE course aims to produce computer professionals who can design, build and operate computer systems and networks, with a thorough knowledge of the basic fundamentals of the internals of the computer hardware and software systems and networks. The CSE course has a higher mathematical content compared to IT.

The Information Technology course is the result of the integration of computer and communication technologies for applications in information processing, design and implementation of IT-enabled services, Internet and Web applications.

Curriculum

A curriculum in CSE / IT contain a core of fundamental material covering algorithms, data structures, software design, concepts of programming languages, computer organization and architecture, operating systems, software methodology and engineering, and theory of computation.

Job Prospects

CSE / IT Graduates are routinely recruited in large numbers major IT companies all over the world. Recruitment for overseas companies is also made very often, as IT profession is the most global in nature. The thrust areas are computerization of financial services, including banking and insurance, production planning and control, design development, management information systems, database management, process management etc. Due to the widespread applications of computers they can find jobs in many industries where computer-aided systems are used. Many software engineers are self-employed and develop computer programs for small establishments.

Aptitude required

IT doesn 't demand much technical aptitude for hardware or lab work and is not of much mathematical nature. One should have good programming logic to be successful in this field. One should also have good capacity for long hours of work and constant updating of knowledge.

At high school level one should have done well in the following areas

- logic
- C, C++

Talent Check

- How did you find your C++ class? Was it intellectually stimulating for you? Were you able to grasp the concepts well?
- While programming at your computer do you get lost in it for hours without feeling bored?
- Get a book of puzzles. Try to solve it. Are you good at it?
- Are you comfortable with working and studying for long hours?

Review

IT is undoubtedly the fastest growing field and provides the highest number of job openings. Fresh graduates and those with little experience can find jobs most easily among the engineering graduates. IT industries also provide the highest starting salaries. Being a global industry IT provides ample scope for executive corporate life style, world class working atmosphere, foreign travel and opportunities to work in North America, Europe, Japan etc, even though opportunities in Middle-East are relatively limited.

However one should also be aware of the challenges that one may face. IT is a highly competitive field, since it is open to anyone with skill. Even non-engineering graduates and engineering graduates in other streams frequently migrate to IT. Despite its expansion it is plainly obvious that IT field will not be able to accommodate all IT job aspirants. The domains change frequently and fast, rendering the learning obsolete and entailing constant updating on the part of the practitioner, which can be quite demanding even for the initiated.

IT usually provides very sedentary jobs which can be quite demanding on psyche and physique, as well one 's social and family life. Jobs are very demanding in terms of working hours and work-pressure, especially for fresh graduates. Due to these reasons IT professionals have the highest burn out rate and for this reason many non-IT graduates are observed not to prefer not to enter this field even after getting selected by prime software companies. And last but not the least, IT field was the most hit by the recent recession.

Comparing CSE and IT Engineering

CSE graduates will fit into any computer organization, including those dealing with computer design and manufacturing, design, installation, operation and maintenance of computer systems and networks, software industries and Internet and web applications.

IT graduates will be suitable for jobs related to information processing, IT-enabled services, providing and development of Internet and web applications.

IT companies have equal preference for both the disciplines if the skill sets of the students fit into their requirements. However, the computer manufacturing industries and Network organisations prefer CSE graduates. Both CSE and IT graduates have equal opportunities to do higher studies at PG and Ph.D. levels.

Comparing Electronics and Communication (ECE) and Computer Science (CSE) branches in terms of suitability for IT field

Both CSE as well as ECE graduates are highly preferred by the IT companies. As against the computer science student who learns only about software, an ECE student is exposed to the hardware part too. However if one is focused on the software field it is better to go for CSE/IT. Computer sciences engineering also has an edge in the form of better placement record in the IT field.

Computer Science & IT Engineering - Synopsis

Aptitude:

- Logic, programming skill, high thinking capacity and concentration.

Positive Aspects:

- Not much technical aptitude for hardware or lab work is required.
- Not very mathematical, in general.
- Highest number of job openings and success rate.
- Fresh graduates can find jobs most easily among the engineering graduates.
- Highest starting salaries.
- One's worth in the job market increases exponentially with experience and skill.
- Highest percentage of graduates employed in the same field of study.
- Good chances for private practice and self employment.
- Provides ample scope for executive corporate life style, world class working atmosphere, foreign travel etc.
- Provides best opportunities to work in North America, Europe, Japan etc, even though opportunities in Middle-East are relatively limited.
- One can diversify into a variety of domains depending upon

one 's aptitude, intellectual capacity and interest.

- Once can grow fast as a programmer, designer, project leader, project manager etc in the corporate ladder.
- The industry-academia gap is narrow compared to other engineering streams.

Negative Aspects:

- A highly competitive field, since IT is open to anyone with skill. Even non-engineering graduates and engineering graduates in other streams frequently migrate to IT.
- IT is not engineering in the true sense of the word since physical phenomena do not come under its scope, but is essentially a study of coding conventions.
- Due to the above reason the IT graduates cannot easily migrate to other engineering fields, even though graduates from other streams can come to IT.
- Qualification in IT does not have much relevance, as the industry looks only for aptitude, skill and experience (even though qualification is crucial at the point of entry to the job-market).
- The domains changes frequently and fast, rendering the learning obsolete.
- Since IT field is fast growing, it entails constant updating on the part of the learner even after graduation, which can be quite demanding even for the initiated.

- Very sedentary job.
- Usually entails work away from your home town, frequent traveling and shifting.
- Very demanding on psyche and physique, especially eyes.
- Very demanding in terms of working hours and work-pressure, especially for fresh graduates.
- Demanding on family and social life, due to the tight time-schedule.
- IT professionals have the highest burn out rate.
- Programming as a long term career option may not be viable to all, even though IT provides for other avenues too.

biotechnology

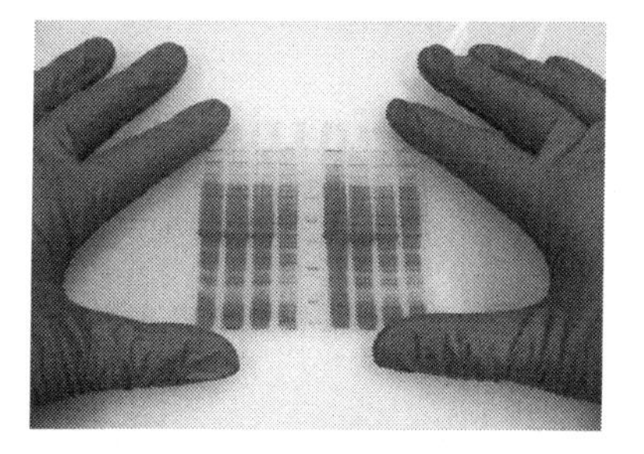

Biotechnology

(B io-Informatics, Biomedical Engineering)

Overview

Bioengineering is a discipline that integrates the engineering sciences with the bio-sciences and clinical practice. Biotechnology has become popular after the manipulation of genes and DNA has been made possible to produce desired products. Ground-breaking developments like Human Genome Project, genetically modified crops and cloning are associated with Bio-engineering. Modern biotechnology involves understanding how life's molecules, such as genes and proteins, interact with one another and are affected by their environment. Biotechnology is an interdisciplinary science that has evolved from and can be combined with various disciplines such as biochemistry, micro-biology, tissue culture and molecular biology.

Biotechnology has current and potential applications in medical field, development of new seeds, environmental pollution control, industries, agriculture, food processing, pharmaceutical, chemical, bio-products, textiles, nutrition and animal science. Biotechnology procedures have wide applications in forensic science, in the detection of criminals or parentage, especially now, with our better understanding of DNA fingerprinting and genetics. Molecular geneticists and technologists are required for understanding the molecular basis of genetic diseases and to find out effective cure. Gene therapy, breeding of new plants and livestock are some of the emerging areas.

Bioinformatics is the advance of Biotechnology which involves utilizing the vast biological databases built over the years by experienced biotechnologists using computer software. Biotechnology requires much database support for genomic and related research. Computational modelling and analysis is now an integral part of the biological discovery process. As geneticists, microbiologists and other researchers continue to gather huge amounts of new information about the human genome and biological molecules, there is a growing demand for sophisticated, computerised approaches for compiling and analysing that data. It has much relevance in pharmaceutical and biotech industries. Bioinformatics combines the tools and techniques of mathematics, computer science and biology in order to understand the biological significance of a given data.

Some of the main areas of bioinformatics are data mining and analysis for genome projects, protein structure prediction, systems biology, developing computer database and algorithms for biological research.

Job prospects for Bioinformatic engineers are mainly in the field of design and implementation of programmes and systems for the storage, management and analysis of biological data, including DNA.

Biomedical engineering combines biology and medicine with engineering to develop devices and procedures that solve medical and health-related problems. Biomedical engineers may be called upon to design instruments and devices, to bring together knowledge from many sources to develop new procedures, or to carry out research to acquire knowledge needed to solve new problems. They develop and evaluate systems and products for use in the fields of biology and health, such as artificial organs, prostheses (artificial devices that replace missing body parts), instrumentation, medical information systems, and health management and care delivery systems.

Job Prospects

Biotechnology engineers are primarily employed in pharmaceutical, medicine manufacturing and medical instruments and supplies industries, in hospitals, in research facilities of educational and medical institutions, and in teaching. In industry Biotechnologists are employed in the areas of chemicals, environment control, waste management, energy, as well as agriculture and food processing industries, besides bioprocess industries. In the public sector there are opportunities in research laboratories run by the government, universities and institutes of technology, agricultural and horticultural institutes, research laboratories, in government regulatory agencies etc.

Curriculum

The Biotechnology curriculum introduces the students to concepts and applications of biochemistry, microbiology, tissue culture, molecular biology, bioinformatics, biomedical engineering, information technology, medical electronics and other advanced topics.

Aptitude Required

One must be interested in biological sciences and also have an engineering bent of mind to take up this course. One should have a good academic record, not necessarily in biotechnology, be strong in the fundamentals of the subject, and have aptitude and can adapt to the changing needs of the field. At the high school level one should do well in the following areas:

- Biology
- Chemistry
- Mathematics
- Electronics

Talent Check

- Did you do well in your high school Biology lab?

- Are you interested in human body and its functioning?
- Do you have any insight into the functioning of living organisms, both plants and animals?
- Are you simultaneously good at Chemistry, Mathematics and Electronics?

Review

Biotechnology is indeed an emerging and promising area. However the career prospects in the Biotechnology field widely varies from country to country. A career in Biotechnology can really be rewarding in countries where there is thriving Biotechnology industry with a good network of research laboratories, rich biodiversity, well developed base industries and rich agriculture sector. The biotechnology professionals can get good jobs in the pharmaceutical companies, agricultural, chemical and allied industries. They can get the employment in the areas of production, planning and management of bio-processing industries. The biotechnologists have a great scope in the research laboratories in various government-based and private universities and research institutes as research scientists or assistants.

However analysts opine that this sunrise industry is not truly career-oriented as far as developing countries are concerned, even though things are changing fast. Hence the potential for jobs in the field of Bioengineering may not be very wide in these countries at the moment, and the career aspirants have to be cautious about this. The research and facilities for Bio-engineering is not well-established in developing countries. Biotechnology industry is risk- oriented and involves lot of finance; huge research platforms are required and returns will take a long time to come. Biotechnology education too is still in infancy there, and even universities and research institutions of repute are groping in the dark as they try to carve out a course and frame syllabus, and initiate the process of preparing the first generation of biotech graduates. Biotech demands a high degree of specialization that can only come with hands-on experience, which limits its appeal only in the destinations of Biotechnology industry.

Biotechnology - Synopsis

Aptitude:

- Cross disciplinary aptitude in Biology/Medical/ Electronics fields.

Positive Aspects:

- An emerging and promising area, especially for those living in or aspiring to work in developed countries.

Negative Aspects:

- Requires cross disciplinary aptitude in a variety of specialties like Electronics, Mechanical and Medical fields.
- Potential for jobs in the field of Bio-engineering field is not very wide in many developing countries at the moment. Fresh graduates will struggle to get a break-through.
- The research and facilities for Bio-engineering is not well-established in such countries.
- The percentage of graduates in Bio-engineering employed in the same field of study is low.
- Graduates are not preferred by IT industry unlike graduates in circuit branches.
- Little opportunities in industries other than pharmaceutical and medical instruments industries.
- The academia-industry gap is very high here, and without

supplementary training and adequate experience the graduate cannot deliver in the field.

- Little chance for private practice.

FAQS

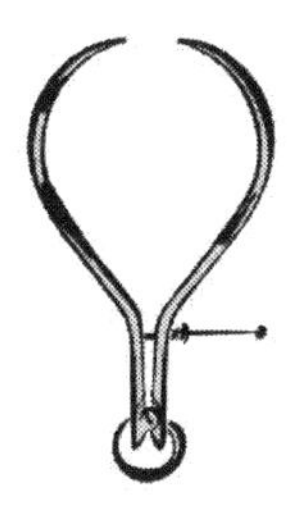

FAQS about engineering

Are all those who have studied engineering happy to be engineers?

Certainly not. There are many cases where even students and graduates from premier engineering colleges soon discover that they were better suited for Law, commerce, management or arts than engineering. Unfortunately, our educational systems don ' t give enough stress on matching the inborn talent of candidates to appropriate professions. So we see many engineering graduates leaving their chosen field to answer their true call later in their career. For those who are not left-brain oriented, or have prodigious talent in any art like writing, singing, public speaking etc, it is better to stay away from engineering.

Do we get to use all that we learn in engineering curriculum in practical life?

Not at all, even assuming one gets to work in industry. One may not get to put in practice even 10% of what one learns in his engineering program. Often engineers start true practical learning only after entering the industry, and get to specialize on just a limited domain.

How should one go on to face the Engineering Counseling?

On the day of the one's appointment during counseling week go to the counseling centre early and keep track of the available seats in the various colleges. When one's turn comes, it is advisable to have a list of groups and colleges one would like to opt for in order of priority. When called for interview to make a choice, inquire if your choice of group and college is available in the order of your preference. Poor planning before the counseling appointment may end up in taking a poor last minute decision.

Between a good branch and a college, which should be given preference?

A "good" branch solely depends on one's aptitude and should be given preference. But any college with good faculty, infrastructure and placement record, in addition to good accreditation, is good enough.

What are the factors I should consider while choosing an engineering institution?

You should consider the following factors:

- Does the college and course have government/university approvals?
- Accreditation rating of the college by foreign universities will be an advantage.
- Infrastructure of the college, especially in your technical interest area.

- The faculty of the college.
- Regularity of classes and track record
- The placement record of the college.
- Links with the industry
- R&D facilities

If possible, visit campuses and talk to professors and students to determine if their institution is for you.

Which are the branches that are more mathematics-oriented and those that are less mathematics-oriented?

Mathematics is a fundamental subject, which encompasses all branches of engineering. Electrical, electronics and communication, civil and mechanical require heavy mathematics orientation while computer science requires the least.

I have no inclination for any particular engineering subject. My main concern is to get a job in my field once I am through my course. Which branch should I choose?

You should go for civil engineering or Computer Science/IT.

Is a good academic record important for a bachelor program in engineering?

Yes. Most Companies specify a cut off percentage of mark to screen the applicants to its posts. It may be aggregate percentage or percentage in each individual semester, and additionally some companies may not want any record of arrears.

Should I study with an objective to score mark, or should I study " for knowledge "?

A direct answer is that you should study for scoring mark. Your academic record is, and is the only, indicator of your knowledge. A good academic record is also a prerequisite for entry to most good jobs, and it goes without saying that the real learning starts only after you have entered the work field.

What should be my academic objectives for my engineering program?

You should aim for the following:

- An aggregate percentage of minimum 70%
- First class in every semester
- No record of arrears
- Qualify for national benchmarks.
- Get campus placement.

How can I achieve a good academic record in my engineering program?

You should follow the following guidelines:

- Be consistent in your studies, even though you need not be a bookworm.

- Be exam-oriented. Study in a manner as to score marks.
- Refer previous question papers to prepare notes and prepare for examinations.
- Submit all assignments.
- Write all examinations and class tests.
- Keep good relations with the teachers and fellow students.

Should I attempt to master all the subjects that are included in my syllabus?

In addition to your core subjects you will also be required to study a variety of other subjects from Physics, Mathematics, Chemistry and other engineering fields. Usually you need, and can, master only your core subjects, which alone will be relevant for your career.

What will define the scope and standard of an engineering curriculum?

The syllabus for national benchmarks (which differs from country to country) is a standard that defines the scope of the curriculum of an engineering field.

How can I enhance my employability and get campus placement?

You can follow these guidelines:

- Register yourselves with placement agencies
- Keep track of and get involved in the activities of the placement

department of your college.

- Keep in contact with the placement officer to know the vacancies and placement drives by companies.
- Take part in all placement drives as far as possible, even if you are not serious about joining, with a focus to gain experience and improve your interview-facing skills and communication abilities.
- Build a network of friends, including in the internet, and share information about jobs.

What are the extra activities I should undertake while studying engineering?

Four years of study in engineering college is a long and crucial period in your life. From day one, a student should focus on improving communication skills, be good at time management, learn to work in a team and carry out multiple tasks. These skills would determine the employability of a candidate and also his suitability for an MBA degree. With this objective follow these guidelines:

- Improve your communication, leadership and presentation skills. Attend language labs if there is one in your college.
- Enhance your interview facing and resume writing skills
- Prepare for tests on abstract reasoning, numerical reasoning, puzzles, English language skills, general knowledge etc,

which will improve your competence for a variety of jobs, including for IT industry.

- As already suggested, constantly improve your knowledge in your field and prepare for national benchmarks.
- You can also start preparing with a long term perspective for engineering jobs in major public sector industries.
- As this is the age of IT, and as IT is the largest job provider to engineering graduates, it is prudent to undertake various computer courses, especially on C and C++.
- Keep a good social profile by socializing with your professional peers. Being a book worm and keeping aloof from all others can prove costly, as it is not *what* you know that often counts, but *who* you know! Associate yourself with Professional organizations and Networks of faculty, students, members of student organizations and working engineers, which can help you to find jobs and get professional advices.
- Attend seminars and present papers at technical festivals.
- If possible also get yourself a mentor who can help you in your career path.

22354994R00071

Made in the USA
Middletown, DE
14 December 2018